*LEGO* **STAR WARS**

# INTRODUCTION

**The rebellious** Separatists cause trouble accross the LEGO® *Star Wars* galaxy. Find out about this dangerous group – from the deadly Destroyer Droid to the beastly Savage Opress.

## HOW TO USE THIS BOOK

These amazing minifigures are ordered according to the *Star Wars*™ property in which they first appeared or mostly featured. Tabs at the top of each page indicate which properties this minifigure appears in. As most *Star Wars* characters appear in the Expanded Universe, that tab is highlighted only if a minifigure appears in an EU set. The Clone Wars tab has not been highlighted if the character has a separate Clone Wars minifigure.

This book also includes variants of featured minifigures, which are the same character, but have some modifications that make them different in some way.

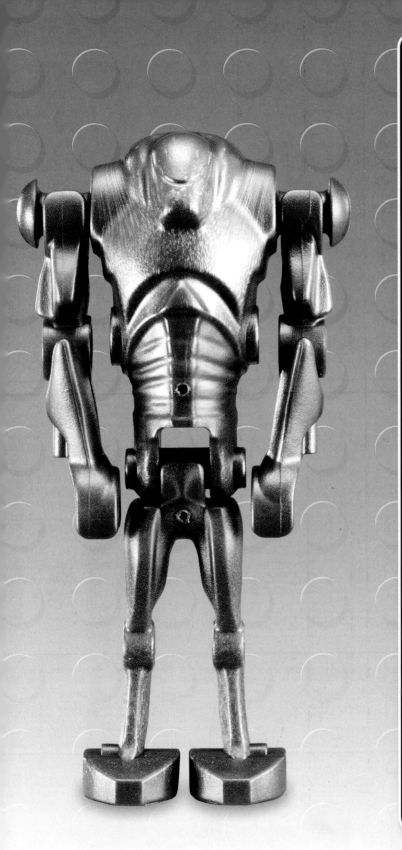

# Contents

**Darth Maul is the** terrifying Sith apprentice of Darth Sidious. Maul wears black robes and a hooded cape as he lurks in the shadows, waiting for his chance to attack the Jedi! Maul's minifigure appears in five LEGO *Star Wars* sets from 1999–2011. The 2011 variant has a unique Zabrak-horned head sculpt and new face and torso patterns.

The 2011 minifigure includes a new mould for Darth Maul's head. This detachable piece features the Zabrak horns that Maul usually hides under his hood

Darth Maul is a Nightbrother from Dathomir. His eyes have turned yellow from studying the dark side

Only one other minifigure wields a double-bladed lightsaber: Savage Opress (p.26)

Updated torso patterns

In the first set to include Darth Maul – Lightsaber Duel (set 7101) – Maul's lightsaber hilt came with only one blade

## DATA FILE
**SET:** 7961 Darth Maul's Sith Infiltrator
**YEAR:** 2011
**PIECES:** 5
**EQUIPMENT:** Double-bladed lightsaber, cape, hood
**VARIANTS:** 3

### Trade Federation MTT (set 7662)

A destroyer droid is delivered in a hulking troop transport along with racks of unfolding battle droids in this 2007 set. It shows the formidable firepower of the Separatist ground forces!

**In 2002, the first** destroyer droid rolled into the world of LEGO *Star Wars*. Also known as a droideka, this robotic ball of firepower is a key part of the Separatists' ground forces. With its distinctive curved spine, the droid posed a challenge to LEGO designers. Two versions were created, the second a more elaborate and complex design.

## STAR VARIANT

### Simple start

The original droideka figure has a much simpler design than the 2007 variant, but its 26 pieces still capture the droid's distinctive shape.

These pieces are also used for battle droids' arms

Blaster energiser

A LEGO Technic piece evenly separates the three legs for stability

Arm section is an adapted hose nozzle piece

Foot piece is used in other LEGO sets as horns on Viking helmets

### DATA FILE

**SET:** 7662 Trade Federation MTT
**YEAR:** 2007
**PIECES:** 35
**EQUIPMENT:** Two blaster energisers
**VARIANTS:** 2

The battle droid minifigure has been released in vast numbers in the LEGO *Star Wars* galaxy, appearing in 27 LEGO sets to date. The Separatist soldier relies on quantity, not skill, to defeat its enemy: It cannot think independently and its firing accuracy is poor – partly because the minifigure could not hold a blaster correctly until 2007!

## Battle Droid
### SEPARATIST FOOT SOLDIER

This LEGO head piece was specially created for the battle droid minifigure

### STAR VARIANTS

**Geonosian**
This variant of the battle droid minifigure appears in Geonosian Fighter (set 4478). It is sand-red instead of tan in colour because it was produced on the planet of Geonosis.

**Backpack**
Two 1999–2000 LEGO sets have included this battle droid with a backpack: Naboo Swamp (set 7121) and the *Star Wars* #4 Battle Droid Minifigure Pack (set 3343).

**Armed arm**
Two variants of the battle droid minifigure can't hold a blaster vertically. However, from 2007 sets onward, the battle droid has had one straight, or turned, arm so the minifigure can hold a gun correctly.

As with normal LEGO minifigures, the battle droid is only articulated at the shoulder, but his two arms are not identical

Regular infantry battle droids have plain tan torsos, but command officers have coloured torsos to denote rank

SE-14 blaster pistol

### DATA FILE
**SET:** 7929 The Battle of Naboo
**YEAR:** 2011
**PIECES:** 5
**EQUIPMENT:** Blaster
**VARIANTS:** 5

The battle droid's feet and legs are one LEGO piece

## DATA FILE

**NAME:** Security droid
**SPECIALTY:** Guard duty
**SET:** 7877 Naboo Starfighter
**YEAR:** 2011
**PIECES:** 5
**EQUIPMENT:** Blaster
**VARIANTS:** 3

Torso piece has dark red markings

**Although all battle** droids are structurally identical and made from the same LEGO pieces, specialist battle droids are fitted with a coloured torso to identify their function. These droids are chosen for certain roles to increase the army's efficiency. They are found in a select few LEGO sets, where their specific skills are required.

The security battle droid has a red tip on the back of its head piece. This head detail is first seen on the 2011 design

### Battle colours
Specialist battle droids have had varying amounts of colour on their torsos since their first release. The earliest variants have mostly tan torsos with small patches of colour, and other variants have full-colour torsos.

The pilot droid is identified by blue markings

Straight arm holds a blaster vertically

## DATA FILE

**NAME:** Pilot droid
**SPECIALTY:** Vehicle handling
**SET:** 7929 The Battle of Naboo
**YEAR:** 2011
**PIECES:** 5
**EQUIPMENT:** Blaster
**VARIANTS:** 3

This variant of the droid commander has an all-yellow torso piece, but a previous variant (seen in two 2000–2002 sets) has a mostly tan torso with yellow markings

## DATA FILE

**NAME:** Droid commander
**SPECIALTY:** Squad leader
**SET:** 7670 Hailfire Droid and Spider Droid
**YEAR:** 2008
**PIECES:** 5
**EQUIPMENT:** Blaster
**VARIANTS:** 2

# Battle Droids
SPECIALISTS

**Bounty hunter** Jango Fett keeps a low profile in the LEGO *Star Wars* galaxy. He is exclusive to one 2002 set: Jango Fett's *Slave I* (set 7153). Jango is made up of many unique LEGO pieces that might make his minifigure as legendary as the man himself, including his two-sided head piece, and helmet with a J-12 jetpack.

### Jango Fett's *Slave I* (set 7153)
Jango Fett's *Slave I* has secret compartments and hidden weapons to aid Jango on his bounty-hunting missions. The ship even has a compartment where Jango's hair and blasters can be stored when he isn't using them.

Jango's black head is visible through the open T-visor of his blue-painted helmet

### Jango's head
One side of Jango's head has a yellow face with a headset and stubble. His black hair can't fit under his helmet.

Torso piece with Mandalorian silver armour plates is unique to Jango

No other LEGO minifigure has these violet arms

Jango's custom-made WESTAR-34 blasters are LEGO revolvers

### Like father...
Jango's J-12 jetpack and helmet are one piece. The adult Boba Fett minifigure wears the same piece in green.

## DATA FILE
**SET:** 7153 Jango Fett's *Slave I*
**YEAR:** 2002
**PIECES:** 4
**EQUIPMENT:** Helmet and jetpack, twin blasters
**VARIANTS:** 1

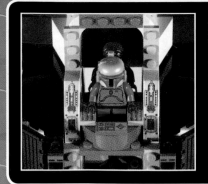

**Jango Fett's**
***Slave I* (set 7153)**
Young Boba Fett sits right behind his father, Jango, in the two-person cockpit of Jango Fett's *Slave I*. When the ship rotates 90 degrees from its horizontal stationary position to its vertical flight mode, the cockpit turns on LEGO Technic axles so the minifigures are always upright. Both young Boba and Jango Fett are exclusive to this 2002 set.

**This determined young** clone will one day become a great bounty hunter, but for now he is learning combat skills under the guardianship of his father, Jango. Young Boba's minifigure is equally as elusive as his father's, appearing in only one set. As he is a child, Boba has short LEGO legs to make him smaller than the Jango minifigure.

## DATA FILE

**SET:** 7153 Jango Fett's *Slave I*
**YEAR:** 2002
**PIECES:** 4
**EQUIPMENT:** None
**VARIANTS:** 1

**Lady locks**
Young Boba's long black hair is typically used on female minifigures. Luke Skywalker and Anakin Skywalker have also been known to sport this hair in LEGO *Star Wars* sets, but only Boba wears it in black.

Boba's unique yellow face with sloping eyebrows and a straight mouth gives him a serious look

This torso piece was specially made for Boba. He wears a v-collared tunic with a drawstring belt

Boba is the only LEGO minifigure to have half-size legs in this medium blue colour

**Boba Fett**
YOUNG CLONE

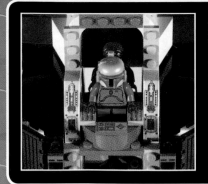

**11**

# Zam Wesell
## BOUNTY HUNTER

**This shady character** has proven elusive in LEGO *Star Wars* and her minifigure is exclusive to one 2002 set. Zam Wesell is a bounty hunter with a special edge: She is a Clawdite shapeshifter who can alter her physical appearance as she chooses. Her minifigure head can change between her pretty human face and her natural Clawdite face!

Podracers Anakin Skywalker and Gasgano also wear these dark grey LEGO flying goggles

### Bounty Hunter Pursuit (set 7133)
Zam flies her nimble airspeeder in just this one 2002 set. The speeder's cockpit has a small control panel for Zam's navigation.

Face veil disguises Zam's human identity

Internal comlink for communicating with associates, including Jango Fett

## DATA FILE
**SET:** 7133 Bounty Hunter Pursuit
**YEAR:** 2002
**PIECES:** 5
**EQUIPMENT:** Projectile rifle
**VARIANTS:** 1

Zam's torso, hips and legs, printed with her specialised armour and equipment, are unique to her minifigure

Zam wears muted sand-purple and silver/grey tones so she can lurk in the shadows undetected

Grappling hook for scaling buildings

### Changeling
Swiveling Zam's head around exposes her true Clawdite form. Zam was one of the first double-faced minifigures.

### Heavy helmet
Zam's face-framing crash helmet is only seen on her minifigure in LEGO *Star Wars*, but it is also used as a heavy-duty helmet (in various colours) by miners in the LEGO themes Rock Raiders and Power Miners. Only Zam wears it in light grey.

## Jedi Duel (set 7103)

Crafty Count Dooku has only ever appeared in this 2002 LEGO set, and he is attempting to make a quick getaway! Dooku has an open-cockpit speeder bike to flee on, but he is forced to duel with Jedi Master Yoda first.

## Curved lightsaber

Count Dooku wields a unique lightsaber with a curved metallic hilt. The piece is exclusive to Count Dooku and it also appears with Dooku's 2009 Clone Wars minifigure in Count Dooku's Solar Sailer (set 7752) (p.21).

**Enigmatic minifigure** Count Dooku was once a Jedi Master, but he has fallen to the dark side. He now lurks in the shadows of the LEGO *Star Wars* galaxy, having remained exclusive to one LEGO set since 2002. As befits a man of Dooku's wealth and status, his minifigure wields a custom-made lightsaber and has a unique head and torso.

Count Dooku's unique head has a grey beard, wrinkled skin and a steely gaze

This is a standard LEGO minifigure cape, but it acts as a symbol of Dooku's prestige as Count of Serenno

Only Count Dooku's minifigure has this torso, adorned with a cape clasp and brown belt

## DATA FILE

**SET:** 7103 Jedi Duel
**YEAR:** 2002
**PIECES:** 5
**EQUIPMENT:** Cape, lightsaber
**VARIANTS:** 1

**Bigger, bulkier and** more bullet-proof than standard battle droids, super battle droids are a force to be reckoned with. Not only are they physically stronger than their spindlier cousins, they also have more brainpower. Three variants of the hulking minifigure have been made – each more intimidating than the last.

# Super Battle Droid
## WALKING WEAPONRY

Specially moulded head-and-body piece is used for all three variants of the super battle droid

**Technical droid**
Like the destroyer droid, the super battle droid has also gone beyond its minifigure beginnings and been created as a LEGO Technic set. The robotic figure, released in 2000, is made from 379 technical parts.

Arms clip to shoulder pieces with same grip as minifigures' hands

## STAR VARIANTS

### Blue beginnings
The first super battle droid minifigure is metal-blue and was released in 2002. Two come with the Republic Gunship (set 7163).

### Blast off
In 2009, the super battle droid swapped one of its arms for a unique piece with a blaster moulded into it. This third variant of the droid appears in two LEGO sets.

Pearlized, dark grey body

Hands can grasp LEGO blaster weapons

## DATA FILE
**SET:** 8091 Republic Swamp Speeder
**YEAR:** 2010
**PIECES:** 4
**EQUIPMENT:** None
**VARIANTS:** 3

Thin legs create a small target for enemy fire

Leg piece is unique to LEGO *Star Wars*. It is also found on the MagnaGuard (p.23) and TX-20 tactical droid (p.25) minifigures

## Geonosian Fighter (set 4478)

In Geonosian Fighter, a Geonosian mans this sonic cannon on a platform that spins 360 degrees and hinges 90 degrees. The set was released in 2003 in a blue box and then in 2004 in a black box.

**2003 saw the** introduction of Geonosian minifigures to the LEGO *Star Wars* theme with two variants of the warrior. The first is a basic drone; the cannon fodder of the Geonosian army. The second is a higher-caste variant with wings. One of each appears in Geonosian Fighter (set 4478).

Monochrome head-mould

## DATA FILE

**SET:** 4478 Geonosian Fighter
**YEAR:** 2003/4
**PIECES:** 4
**EQUIPMENT:** Blaster
**VARIANTS:** 2

The two Geonosian warrior minifigures are identical except for the addition or omission of the orange wings

Plastic wings in two parts are unique to LEGO *Star Wars*

Sonic blaster fires concussive energy

The rocky outcrops of Geonosis house the hive colonies of an insectoid, hive-minded race, which is loyal to the Separatist cause. This 2011 Geonosian minifigure pilots a starfighter at the Battle of Geonosis. It has unique torso and leg printings and an all-new head shape that develops the original LEGO Geonosian head-mould.

**Geonosian Starfighter (set 7959)**
This set, which exclusively features the 2011 Geonosian pilot minifigure, revisits the Geonosian starfighter model from 2003. The ships are flown by Geonosian pilots in the Battle of Geonosis.

Insectoid eyes bulge out of new head-mould

The second Geonosian head-mould has a more defined shape and new coloured detail

Geonosian exoskeleton markings

Chitin armour, with its composition of insect shell and animal skin, protects against the sonic energy weapons favoured by Geonosians

Gold markings are typical of Geonosian decoration

Red iketa stones are symbols of war in Geonosian culture

## DATA FILE
**SET:** 7959 Geonosian Starfighter
**YEAR:** 2011
**PIECES:** 3
**EQUIPMENT:** None
**VARIANTS:** 1

## General Grievous's Starfighter (set 8095)

The Clone Wars General Grievous minifigure is exclusive to this set. His luxurious starfighter includes a medical room, lightsaber rack, an opening cockpit with controls, and hidden missiles.

**General Grievous's cyborg** minifigure has been updated for a 2010 LEGO Clone Wars appearance. His four-armed minifigure is now built entirely from exclusive pieces! Grievous is still a vicious villain with an untempered hatred of the Jedi and a ghastly lightsaber collection, but his menacing minifigure is now one-of-a-kind.

Grievous's rotting red and yellow eyes are printed on his head piece. The classic Grievous minifigure has no face printing (p.28)

Grievous's four arms have hinged joints so they can be positioned in many ways

Grievous collects the lightsabers of his Jedi victims

### Not a droid

Grievous hates being called a droid. He is a cyborg: part flesh, part metal. Grievous's classic minifigure (p.28) is built from some droid parts, but his Clone Wars minifigure is completely unique – something Grievous would probably approve of.

### DATA FILE

**SET:** 8095 General Grievous' Starfighter
**YEAR:** 2010
**PIECES:** 8
**EQUIPMENT:** Four lightsabers, blaster
**VARIANTS:** 1

Dark bluish-grey and tan colours are new to this Grievous minifigure

# General Grievous
## CLONE WARS CYBORG

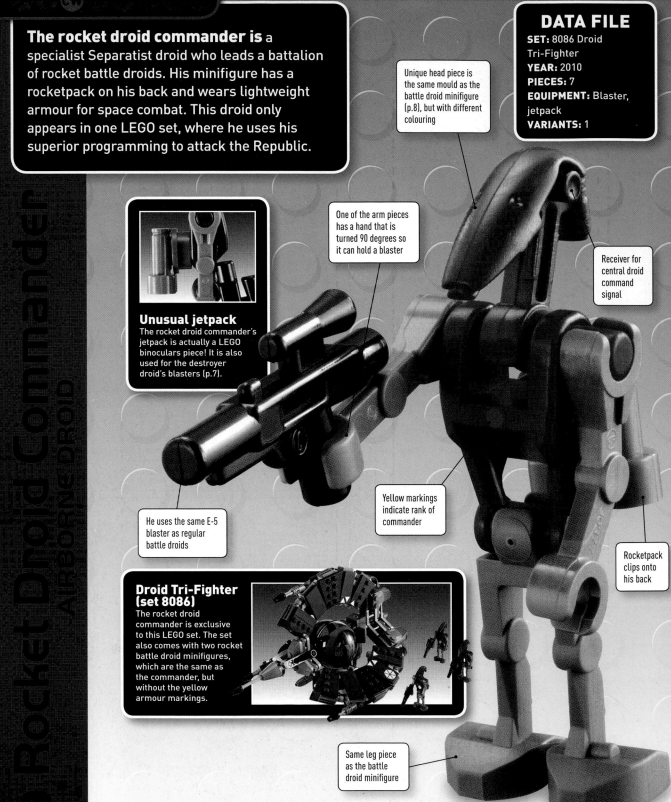

# Rocket Droid Commander
## AIRBORNE DROID

**The rocket droid commander is** a specialist Separatist droid who leads a battalion of rocket battle droids. His minifigure has a rocketpack on his back and wears lightweight armour for space combat. This droid only appears in one LEGO set, where he uses his superior programming to attack the Republic.

## DATA FILE
**SET:** 8086 Droid Tri-Fighter
**YEAR:** 2010
**PIECES:** 7
**EQUIPMENT:** Blaster, jetpack
**VARIANTS:** 1

Unique head piece is the same mould as the battle droid minifigure (p.8), but with different colouring

One of the arm pieces has a hand that is turned 90 degrees so it can hold a blaster

Receiver for central droid command signal

### Unusual jetpack
The rocket droid commander's jetpack is actually a LEGO binoculars piece! It is also used for the destroyer droid's blasters (p.7).

Yellow markings indicate rank of commander

He uses the same E-5 blaster as regular battle droids

Rocketpack clips onto his back

### Droid Tri-Fighter (set 8086)
The rocket droid commander is exclusive to this LEGO set. The set also comes with two rocket battle droid minifigures, which are the same as the commander, but without the yellow armour markings.

Same leg piece as the battle droid minifigure

Orange head sensors enable the elite assassin droid to see in all directions at once

**The elite assassin droid** is the best of the best. Encased in black armour, this skilled assassin can blend into the shadows during a top-secret mission. His tall, thin minifigure has appeared in three LEGO sets since 2009 – always in the unsavoury company of bounty hunters or other assassin droids.

### Bounty Hunter Assault Gunship (set 7930)
The elite assassin droid joins bounty hunters Embo, Aurra Sing and Sugi on board the assault gunship. This villainous group are on the hunt for Jedi, who they can capture and lock up in the ship's prison cell.

Cone head piece is unique to assassin droids in LEGO *Star Wars*

Assassin droid has the same torso piece as the battle droid minifigure (p.8) and rocket droid commander (opposite)

### DATA FILE
**SET:** 7930 Bounty Hunter Assault Gunship
**YEAR:** 2011
**PIECES:** 8
**EQUIPMENT:** Blaster rifle
**VARIANTS:** 1

His body is covered with blaster-proof armour

Long-range blaster rifle is perfect for carrying out assassinations without being detected

### Assassin droid
The regular assassin droid minifigure is exactly the same as the elite assassin droid, apart from his colour. The assassin droid is silver, and comes in just one LEGO set, Assassin Droids Battle Pack (set 8015). One of the more famous assassin droids is IG-88.

**Asajj Ventress is a** deadly assassin who works for the Sith Lord Count Dooku. Her fearsome minifigure has a unique head, torso and legs, and wields twin red-bladed lightsabers. Asajj has dark side powers and a fiery temper – and she is on a mission to cause trouble for the Jedi in two LEGO Clone Wars sets.

### Extra printing
As well as her tattoo markings, Asajj Ventress's sleeveless body suit armour printing also continues on to the back of her torso piece. The 2008 variant doesn't have printing on the back.

Asajj's Sith training gives her expert lightsaber skills

# Asajj Ventress
## SITH ASSASSIN

Purple tattoo markings are continued on the back of the head

Unique head piece is printed with tattoos, which are in memory of Asajj's former master, Ky Narec

Unique torso is printed with Asajj's grey and black body suit and the top of her blue, flowing skirt

Asajj wields a red lightsaber. The curved hilt is unique to her minifigure in LEGO *Star Wars*

## DATA FILE
**SET:** 7957 Dathomir Speeder
**YEAR:** 2011
**PIECES:** 3
**EQUIPMENT:** Twin lightsabers
**VARIANTS:** 2

### Change of clothes
Asajj also appears in the 2008 LEGO set Republic Attack Gunship (set 7676). Her minifigure still carries deadly twin lightsabers, but she is dressed in a different outfit with a unique torso and black cloth skirt.

## Count Dooku's Solar Sailer (set 7752)

Count Dooku's Clone Wars minifigure is exclusive to this set, which also features his solar sailer ship and small, one-seater speeder bike (pictured). The solar sailer has a secret cargo bay in which the speeder can be hidden when Count Dooku isn't using it.

**Count Dooku is the** powerful leader of the Separatists – but he is also a Sith Lord! His Clone Wars minifigure is dressed in dark colours, with a cape and hood, so he can carry out secret missions in shadowy corners of the LEGO *Star Wars* galaxy. Dooku's mysterious minifigure only appears in one set.

Red lightsaber blades are only used by the Sith

Unique face is printed with hooded eyes and wrinkles that are a result of Dooku's dark side training

Dooku's unique torso is printed with a brown belt and an ornate cape chain clasp

Dooku's special curved lightsaber hilt also comes with the classic Count Dooku minifigure (p.13)

## DATA FILE

**SET:** 7752 Count Dooku's Solar Sailer
**YEAR:** 2009
**PIECES:** 5
**EQUIPMENT:** Lightsaber, cape, hood
**VARIANTS:** 1

**Hooded villain**
As well as his grey hair piece, Count Dooku comes with a brown hood so he can travel and cause trouble in disguise.

21

Count Dooku's personal pilot droid is the only one of his kind in LEGO *Star Wars*, but he is entirely made up of LEGO pieces seen on other minifigures. His body is made from battle droid parts, and his head is seen on skeletons in other LEGO themes, including Fantasy Era. The FA-4 model droid exclusively pilots Count Dooku's Solar Sailer (set 7752).

### Count Dooku's Solar Sailer (set 7752)
The pilot droid sits on a sliding seat inside the working cockpit of Count Dooku's *Punworcca 116*-class interstellar sloop. He navigates through a rounded cockpit window.

Rounded head piece has ridges on the other side

### Leg head
The pilot droid's head can be found on many other minifigures, but it has never before been used as a head piece – it mostly functions as a leg piece on LEGO skeletons.

This white mechanical torso piece is commonly used on battle droids (pp.8-9)

General Grievous (p.28) has these same white mechanical arms, but his minifigure has four of them!

Some FA-4 pilot droids move around on wheels, but the LEGO FA-4 has white mechanical legs

## Pilot Droid
### COUNT DOOKU'S CHAUFFEUR

### DATA FILE
**SET:** 7752 Count Dooku's Solar Sailer
**YEAR:** 2009
**PIECES:** 5
**EQUIPMENT:** None
**VARIANTS:** 1

## MagnaGuard Starfighter (set 7673)

Two MagnaGuards appear in this 2008 set. Their specialised starfighter has deadly flick-fire missiles. The MagnaGuards store their electrostaffs at the back of the ship's wings during flight.

**The MagnaGuard** minifigure is an advanced battle droid designed by General Grievous to pose a threat to any clone troopers or Jedi Knights that cross his path. Dressed to intimidate in a unique Kaleesh warrior headwrap and cape, the MagnaGuard carries an impenetrable electrostaff that is resistant to lightsaber blades.

Glowing red photoreceptors

Only the MagnaGuard minifigure carries a powerful LEGO electrostaff

Headwrap is integrated in the MagnaGuard's unique head piece

Torso piece was first seen on the MagnaGuard. Fellow Separatist droid A4-D (p.27) adopted it in 2010

Mechanical arm is in two parts

## DATA FILE

**SET:** 7752 Count Dooku's Solar Sailer
**YEAR:** 2009
**PIECES:** 9
**EQUIPMENT:** Cape, electrostaff
**VARIANTS:** 1

This large red round plate piece is a second photoreceptor

## Cruel cape

The MagnaDroid is the only LEGO minifigure to feature this tan cloth cape with a tattered edge.

The super battle droid (p.14) and TX-20 (p.25) have the same mechanical legs

# MagnaGuard
## MECHANICAL MONSTER

**As the Viceroy** of the Trade Federation, Nute Gunray has a lot of power. But instead of working for the good of the LEGO *Star Wars* galaxy, this Neimoidian minifigure is motivated by greed. Nute's well-dressed but miserable minifigure is the only Neimoidian to have been created in LEGO bricks. He appears in just one set.

Elaborate Neimoidian headdress

### Separatist Shuttle (set 8036)
Nute is a cowardly minifigure. On a mission to meet Senator Onaconda Farr in this set, Nute travels with two battle droid guards, and hides in a secret chamber on board the shuttle.

Nute's head piece is printed with his mottled, grey Neimoidian skin – and his perpetual frown

Iron deposits build up in Neimoidians, turning their eyes orange

Nute's elaborate official robes are printed on his unique torso

Metal badge in the shape of the official Trade Federation insignia

Grey, scaly Neimoidian hands

Nute's Viceroy robes are bright in colour so he gets more attention than lesser officials

## Nute Gunray
### TRADE FEDERATION VICEROY

### DATA FILE
**SET:** 8036 Separatist Shuttle
**YEAR:** 2009
**PIECES:** 4
**EQUIPMENT:** None
**VARIANTS:** 1

The TX-20 is much more intelligent than his battle droid counterpart

**Tactical Droid TX-20** is a strategic planner and supervisor of Separatist troops stationed in Ryloth City. His unique minifigure made his debut in the 2011 LEGO Clone Wars set Mace Windu's Jedi Starfighter (set 7876). He has an unusual combined head-and-torso piece that is exclusive to his minifigure.

Unique Separatist symbol

## DATA FILE
**SET:** 7868 Mace Windu's Jedi Starfighter
**YEAR:** 2011
**PIECES:** 4
**EQUIPMENT:** None
**VARIANTS:** 1

Processing unit buried inside heavily armoured torso to protect it when under fire from enemy forces

Dark blue mechanical arm exclusive to TX-20

Legs are also seen on the super battle droid (p.14) and MagnaGuard (p.23) minifigures

**Mace Windu's Jedi Starfighter (set 7868)**
The tactical droid zips around on his Separatist Flitknot speeder. He has a seat that allows him to comfortably perch and then jump out when he needs to.

**Savage Opress is** on a secret mission. Hired by Asajj Ventress to destroy Count Dooku, his minifigure poses as Dooku's new apprentice. Savage appears in just one LEGO set, where his horned, Dathomirian minifigure must decide who to attack: the Jedi Anakin Skywalker, or his two despised Sith masters?

## Savage Opress
### DARK APPRENTICE

**Dathomir Speeder (set 7957)**
Asajj Ventress, a Nightsister from Savage's home planet of Dathomir, pilots a Nightspeeder with Savage in this set.

LEGO spear piece with axe head attached

Enchanted blade is a weapon from a clan of witches called the Nightsisters

Savage's Zabrak head piece is the same mould as Darth Maul's horned head piece (p.6), but with yellow markings in a different pattern

Savage's fellow Dathomirian, Darth Maul, is the only other minifigure to wield a double-bladed lightsaber

Yellow Nightbrother tattoos

Unique armour piece fits over the minifigure's neck. The Dathomirian armour protects Savage's torso and shoulders

## DATA FILE
**SET:** 7957 Dathomir Speeder
**YEAR:** 2011
**PIECES:** 5
**EQUIPMENT:** Double-bladed lightsaber, enchanted blade
**VARIANTS:** 1

### General Grievous' Starfighter (set 8095)

A4-D ensures that General Grievous's cyborg body is well maintained in this LEGO set. The medical room has a swivelling chair and a rack for Grievous's large lightsaber collection.

**A4-D is a sadistic** medical droid and General Grievous's personal doctor in just one LEGO set. His minifigure is built out of standard droid parts, but with many medical modifications! Extra arms on A4-D's torso hold all manner of equipment, which he is more than happy to use – no matter how much pain he causes!

Sticker is printed with A4-D's logic centre

Surgical laser helps A4-D perform operations with precision

Device contains fluid for use during an operation. It is attached to an arm on A4-D's back

Gripping tool holds Grievous steady during a procedure

Electric saw is actually a LEGO zip-line handle

Leg piece is also used for battle droids (p.8)

30376 5-02

## A4-D

### SADISTIC ROBOT DOCTOR

### DATA FILE

**SET:** 8095 General Grievous' Starfighter
**YEAR:** 2010
**PIECES:** 18
**EQUIPMENT:** Tools
**VARIANTS:** 2

**This vicious cyborg** might look like a LEGO droid, but don't tell him that! He will react savagely, as his many victims will attest. General Grievous is Supreme Commander of the Droid Armies. His minifigure has four lightsabers – two blue and two green – to fill his four arms, making him more than a match for any Jedi!

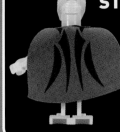
## DATA FILE
**SET:** 7656 General Grievous Starfighter
**YEAR:** 2007
**PIECES:** 7
**EQUIPMENT:** Blaster, four lightsabers
**VARIANTS:** 2

General Grievous's head-mould was specially created for his minifigure

Skull-like mask contains the cyborg's eyes and brain

General Grievous hates to be called a droid, so he won't be pleased that his LEGO arm pieces are also used on 20 LEGO *Star Wars* droids!

General Grievous carries a blaster as well as four lightsabers in General Grievous' Starfighter (set 7656)

### General Grievous Chase (set 7255)
General Grievous entered LEGO *Star Wars* sets astride his imposing wheel-bike. He is being chased by General Obi-Wan Kenobi, who is on a giant varactyl lizard in this 2005 set – the first to feature Grievous. The bike has two pairs of legs to help him hot-foot it out of trouble!

## Droid Tri-Fighter (set 7252)

The buzz droid makes its first appearance in this 2005 set. The minifigure is housed within the central sphere of this deadly LEGO Droid Tri-Fighter, ready to be unleashed during a space dog fight!

**Look out for** this deadly LEGO buzz droid! Unleashed by the Separatists, this droid attaches itself to enemy starships with its legs and then destroys them with a powerful circular saw. The minifigure has wreaked havoc in three LEGO sets.

Shock-absorbing outer hull. This piece is also used for astromech droid heads in LEGO *Star Wars*, though with different printing

Buzz droids have primary and secondary photoreceptors for homing in on targets

Inbuilt circular saw destroys starships

### DATA FILE

**SET:** 7751 Ahsoka's Starfighter and Vulture Droid
**YEAR:** 2009
**PIECES:** 13
**EQUIPMENT:** Built-in circular saw
**VARIANTS:** 1

These mechanical legs are seen on battle droids (p.8) and other droid minifigures in LEGO *Star Wars*

29

Penguin Random House

**Editors** Hannah Dolan, Shari Last, Victoria Taylor and Matt Jones
**Designers** Anne Sharples and Jon Hall
**Senior Producer** Lloyd Robertson
**Senior DTP Designer** David McDonald
**Managing Editor** Simon Hugo
**Design Manager** Guy Harvey
**Creative Manager** Sarah Harland
**Art Director** Lisa Lanzarini
**Publisher** Julie Ferris
**Publishing Director** Simon Beecroft

Additional minifigures photographed by Huw Millington, Ace Kim, Jeremy Beckett and Tony Wood

First published in Great Britain
by Dorling Kindersley Limited,
80 Strand, London, WC2R 0RL

Contains material previously published in
LEGO® Star Wars™ Character Encyclopedia (2011)

001-290606-Aug/15

Page design copyright ©2015 Dorling Kindersley Limited
A Penguin Random House Company

A CIP catalogue record for this book
is available from the British Library

ISBN: 978-0-2412-4771-6

Printed in China

Dorling Kindersley would like to thank:
Jonathan W. Rinzler, Troy Alders, Rayne Roberts, Pablo
Hidalgo, and Leland Chee at Lucasfilm; Stephanie
Lawrence, Randi Sørensen, Lisbeth Langjkær, Jens
Kronvold Frederiksen, Chris Bonven Johansen, and John
McCormack at the LEGO Group; LEGO Star Wars
collectors Ace Kim and Huw Millington; Emma Grange,
Lisa Stock, Sarah Harland, Ellie Hallsworth, and Nicola
Brown for editorial support; and Owen Bennett for
design support on the cover.

www.LEGO.com
www.starwars.com
www.dk.com

A WORLD OF IDEAS:
SEE ALL THERE IS TO KNOW